All in Measure
A Book of Hours
2020-2022

Heather Saunders Estes

San Francisco | Fairfield | Delhi

All In Measure
Heather Saunders Estes

Copyright ©2023 by Heather Saunders Estes

First Edition.

ISBN: 978-1-4218-3532-7

Library of Congress Cataloging-in-Publication Data

All rights reserved. Printed in the United States of America. No part of this book may be used or reproduced in any manner whatsoever without written permission except in the case of brief quotations embodied in critical articles and reviews. For information contact:

Author Photo: C. Rutter

1ST WORLD LIBRARY
PO Box 2211
Fairfield, Iowa 52556
www.1stworldpublishing.com

BLUE LIGHT PRESS
www.bluelightpress.com
Email: bluelightpress@aol.com

*For My Chosen Family
and Friends*

Thank you for your companionship,
love, kindness,
and willingness to learn and change with me.

Praying For Apples — Dawn

Give Us a Sign — Morning

Know My Place — Noon

Blue-Lavender — Afternoon

Howling Up the Hillside — Dusk

Diving Toward the Horizon — Evening

Unspoken Midnight — Dark

Table of Content

Introduction   xi

Praying for Apples — Dawn   1
   Almost Winter Solstice   3
   Supplication   5
   Choices and Omens   6
   Above The Din   7
   Double Suns   8
   Stitching Our Family Together   9
   Paperwhite Narcissus   10
   Praying for Apple   12
   Message   13

Give Us a Sign — Morning   15
   Mont Saint-Michel — 2022   17
   Any Day Now   19
   A Girl's Best Friend   20
   Illuminated   21
   Observance — Easter, 2020   23
   It's a kind of desire   25
   Rain   26
   Starting A Quarantine Project   28
   My Daughter Sleeps a Lot   30
   Give Us a Sign   31
   Hawk Shadow   32
   Duty Calls   33
   Jasmine Tea   35

Know My Place — Noon   37
- *Inauguration — January 20, 2021*   39
- *Self-Quarantine — February, 2020*   40
- *Border Skirmishes*   41
- *Neighbor Kids With Screwdrivers*   44
- *Ties That Bind*   45
- *I was the person at the wedding*   47
- *Fox News, 2020*   49
- *Annunciation*   51
- *Revelation*   52
- *The Guardian*   53

Blue-Lavender — Afternoon   55
- *What's Next for Me?*   57
- *A Welcome Visitor*   58
- *My Chinese Elm Bonsai Is Family*   60
- *Grandmother*   62
- *Retrospective: Pandemic Days*   64
- *Breaker Zone*   65
- *Grace*   66
- *On Our Forty-Ninth Wedding Anniversary, We Do Family Therapy*   67
- *Air Under Our Wings*   69
- *Did the Scrub Jay Notice?*   70
- *Enough*   71
- *Tea Ceremony*   72

Howling Up the Coastline — Dusk   75
   I Am a Big Woman Shopping for Bras   77
   Island of My Body   79
   Cutting My Husband's Hair   80
   Carquinez Strait   81
   The Days of Crows   82
   Glen Canyon Park   83
   Metamorphosis   85

Diving Toward the Horizon — Evening   87
   The Young Man Who Died   89
   I Thought I Was Immune to the Fires — Living in the City   90
   Just For the Night   92
   Joy Fishing —   94
   Hope Is a Winged Thing   94
   The Earth Can Outwait Us   96
   Invitation   97
   We Imagine Cocktail Bars and Toast Ourselves Around the Dining Table   98
   Never Too Old   100
   Haibun for Arachnids   101
   The secret of the universe   102
   Turning Seventy   103

Unspoken Midnight — Dark   105
   Strait of Juan de Fuca — Port Angeles, Washington   107
   Swan Valley, Wyoming   109
   Does My Lineage End If My Only Child Has No Children?   110
   Red-Tailed Hawk   111

Babel   112
Deep Night   113
Midnight Meadow   114
Teton Range: Wyoming Winter   115
Ode to Doughnuts   116
A Quiet Edge   118
Messengers or Prophets?   119
Bodies in Conjunction   121

Acknowledgments   122

About the Author   123

Introduction

This book is inspired by the tradition of praise, contemplation and prayer found in the medieval Books of Hours. These small books were commissioned and used by wealthy, medieval women and are often beautifully illuminated. The printing press made simpler and less expensive copies more available starting in the 1500's. Their contents have varied over 2000 years of Christianity. They include readings of psalms and other writings by day and season and sometimes are personalized. The devotionals are read at specified times, flowing from a more ancient Jewish tradition. Traditionally, there are seven or eight readings a day, but there can be as few as Morning and Evening — Matins and Vespers.

Throughout the centuries, variations on the "Little Office of the Blessed Virgin Mary" continued an emphasis on the use of these books by secular women. Eastern Orthodox, Anglican and other related religions have their own adaptations. Rilke was inspired by these beautiful books in his *Book of Hours: Love Poems to God*. W.H. Auden, very interested in Episcopalian prayer books, participated in a new translation of the psalms. He then wrote seven poems as part of his own, *Horae Canonicae*. Thomas Merton wrote poems/prayers that were collected into a *Book of Hours* edited by Kathleen Deignan. Merton's book is divided into Dawn, Day, Dusk and Dark. Kevin Young created a marvelous *Book of Hours* in 2014.

As we shelter-in-place during the waves of the COVID pandemic, I feel a kinship with hermits, monks and other cloistered souls. Having retired from a very busy and public career a few years earlier, I feel the seclusion dramatically. My husband has been at home writing and teaching on-line during this time. Our twenty-something daughter, and probably the rest of the household, caught

COVID in mid-February, 2020, before testing, vaccines or even common understanding of the infection. She has been living with fatigue and other symptoms of long COVID since — slowly getting better. Our sicknesses meant we all hunkered down with fevers and coughing in February and early March 2020, overlapping with the first shelter-in-place regulations in San Francisco. My husband, daughter, our Gen Z family friend, and I have been living in virtual hibernation.

The days in our house on a hill have assumed a character of ritual and seclusion. These poems chronicle my gratitude, fears and contemplations during this unusual time. My beliefs about the importance of appreciation, while more pagan and idiosyncratic than the original spiritual history and guidance of the Books of Hours, share a common core of praise and valuing the diversity of life and the universe.

We become so accustomed to you,
we no longer look up
when your shadow falls over the book we are reading
and makes it glow.

> From Rainer Maria Rilke's *Book of Hours: Love Poems to God*
> — Translated by Anita Barrows and Joanna Macy

Praying for Apples — Dawn

Almost Winter Solstice

Hush from the thick blanket of fog
seeps through the bedroom curtains.
Moisture from trees like melting snow.
The room is still dark
as sleep begins to drift away.
It is quiet; then I hear again the rumble
and drive gears of snow plows.

Warm in the down comforter,
I snuggle in deeper, but sense
far away, a sleigh-bell?
Maybe the snow will be so deep
with the plows busy early.
I turn toward my warm husband.
The light at the window edges
is just graying, opaque from snowfall.

Surfacing from the sleep-ocean,
a garbage truck's back-up beep
unsettles me in time.
I awaken in my single four poster,
the family dog asleep on the bearskin rug.

I hear the rattle and bang
of the iron hot water radiator,
my blue mittens, almost dry, nearby.
Arm around my pink stuffed pig
with the gingham snout.

Catching my breath, I am lost in place and time.
My mind runs through different bedrooms
searching the clues
of my mother's Queen Anne chair,
the tall windows.

It is the right time of year, almost the solstice —
sixty years, eleven other bedrooms,
and a continent away.
My husband, still asleep, reaches for me.

Supplication

Open the blinds to each morning's revelation
of sky, fog, clouds and colors over hills.
Oolong tea and the scent of rosemary
on my fingers in the garden.
Relax into a strong hug.

I seem to pray in appreciation, gratitude, love —
not out of desperation or need.
Would my life change if I petitioned
the universe for help?
I seek the few stars I can see in the city
for reassurance of continuity,
existence and beauty.

Who do I think will answer?
Who or what is this goddess I give jasmine
or red geraniums to each morning?
My ancestors?
Self love?

My faith has not yet been tested.
I live a charmed life. Not perfect,
but what I can handle.
My poems are offerings of thanks,
not requests.
I pray it will stay that way.

Choices and Omens

Every pandemic morning, she and I go out for coffee.
Drive to the intersection of five roads and pause,
rarely other early traffic, so we can stop,
consider the options. Right? Left?
Old faithful or the friendly barista who knows us by name?
The shop that offers nitro cold-brew or oolong latte?
Perhaps the coffee shop near the bakery
with eclairs and chive cheddar scones.
Longer ride or quicker?
Coffee that makes us growl?
Or giggle?

Destination set, music choices must fit
the tenor of the morning.
Lately it has been "Walpurgasnicht" sung in German
which neither of us understand —
Skrillex, Simon and Garfunkel, or Black Pink.

Back up our hill to turn into the driveway,
we are faced with the final omen of the journey —
will the garage door opener work?
If it opens on the first press, will it be a good day?
Or will its recalcitrance foreshadow difficulties?

We repeat our set patterns,
manage through ritual,
talking to the garage door opener.
Hope to keep our hope, celebrate our small choices.

Above The Din

I begin the morning ritual
by leaning out my third story deck railing
to survey the little valley below —
Twin Peaks beyond. Far away
see sunrise and the cup of blue Bay
between hills and trees.
This is the top of my world.
To the north — a piece of downtown,
the tip of the Salesforce mackerel.
To the west — Angel Island, Point Richmond,
Golden Gate towers.
Toward the Pacific,
Farallon Islands and sunset.

Our house is higher on a San Francisco hill.
Ravens and wild parrots
wing through the day at eye-level,
fire engines, buses below.
The umbrella of sky above.
Colors illuminated in catches of sun,
shadowed by rushing clouds or fog.

Evening settles, I step out again
onto the cool deck.
Breathe in
the dark, dark.

Double Suns

Another smoke-filled sunrise,
the sun, fuchsia red.
Below, a trick reflection in the bay,
another sun — squat like a lump
of red bean paste
but hot-eyed and wavering.

Stitching Our Family Together

Mom sewed cotton shirts and shifts,
and my turquoise linen wedding dress.
I created patchwork story quilts.
She always begged me
to help her thread the needle
on the ancient, faithful Singer.

Last time I followed a sewing pattern
was forty-nine years ago.
I have a new machine now, all digital.
My daughter designs dancing skirts for friends.
I cut rectangles for masks
from fabric with pink elephants.

Even with two pairs of reading glasses,
one on top of the other,
lights turned up, I can barely see
the needle's eye.
I call my daughter.

We sew masks with stars and strawberries,
black squares for her friend, blue fish for her dad.
I am vindicated for hoarding
old sheets, t-shirts, ribbons and bandanas.
We clothe their faces and manage their fates.

Paperwhite Narcissus

Only water is required
for the bulb to build root threads.
The roots coil and tangle,
thin worms in the glass vase,
pale, like something beneath the ground.

Growing in silence, in dark.
Weeks pass. A white nub
pushes through the bulb's onion skin.
Knows its blind way up to the sky.

Nub becomes a sprout, a spear, blanched stems.
Out in sunlight, chloroplasts
green the stalks.

Buds swells.
Butterflies of petals strain
against the translucent, green skin,
moving, shifting, turning.

Morning releases more petals
and powerful perfume
to call dreaming bees, and me.
I lean into the flowers,
close my eyes.

Every winter, in the still dark days,
I participate in this ritual of hope.
Outside, deep in the cold earth, other bulbs
are wrapped in slow sleep.

Praying for Apple

> *From China, it says on the back in my mother's handwriting,*
> *Aspara — Angels of Buddha.*

On the wall, the golden foil cutout
of a flying, smiling goddess
lightly touches down on turquoise-blue felt
inside the gilt bamboo frame.
Her patterned silk robes balloon
in the atmospheric breezes between clouds.
Ample breasts swathed only in gauze.
It is chilly in the sky.
One arm is raised in a jaunty salute,
the other seems to effortlessly hold
what appears to be a golden pie.
A supernatural baker with pie-making
skills of my mother-in-law!
She gently alights outside on the deck,
anklets jingling on her bare feet.
I rush to her in welcome.

Message

> *"Inscribe my name in the book of waves."*
> — Edward Hirsch

My daughter's fifth grade green-glazed handprint tile
is part of the wall of her middle school.
I gave back the clay sculptures I made in college.
Hid them in the forest behind campus,
tucked under pine branches,
on my graduation day.
Thanked the earth for its loan.

Neighbors piece together fairy cottages and altars
at the base of the largest Monterey cypress
across the street in the city park.
They leave little plastic horses, daisy rings, photos.
Prayers rise into the sighing branches
for the ravens to carry.

Give Us a Sign — Morning

Mont-Saint-Michel — 2022

Four seekers here,
each behind a closed door —
monks in rows of humble cells,
damp wool, wind drafts chill
off the hewn stone.
Each toiling in vineyards of mind.

I tap letters into prayers.
Design creatures in Eden, trees, ivy and stars.
Inscribe them in ink with a crow quill.
Lick my brush, dip it in crushed lapis,
and gold ink to illuminate my visions.

Scarlet yarns, cloak blue, moss green
pull like rosaries through fingers.
She weaves a mantra of minutes and hours.
Her prayer wheel of consciousness whirls
as she meditates.

A teacher, scholar, and chronicler
sits in blue pools of papers.
Bulwarks of books surround the floor.
Ideas circle and swirl.

The fourth on our fog shrouded island
seeks order and balance
learning languages, translating ancient texts,
searching for secrets and meaning.

We are cloistered but not ascetics.
Korean, and Thai food, twelve-layer
Russian honey cakes are carted
across the city to our hilltop fortress.
In seclusion, we contemplate our works,
ocean, waves, and sky.

For each monk and scribe who illuminated
the intricate Books of Hours,
many more grazed sheep, tilled fields,
tithed from their meager crops.

Essential workers risk their lives
as we sit safe and secure in our home
luxuriating in this forced quietude.
Medieval inequity was stark and cruel.
So it is in our pandemic world.

Any Day Now

That cough —
Covid-19 beginning?
Am I hot? Tired?
Tired of cleaning.
I forget for hours at a time
that I am waiting
to get sick.
Inevitable,
or so they say.
In the meantime,
my personal curves
are not flattening.
My hair has lengthened
along with the days.

I have rechecked my will.
Told my husband and daughter
I love them.
Better to be prepared
than caught in denial.

The sun shines warm
as I curl on the blue rug
in the dusty beams of the moment
and nap a cat's dream.

A Girl's Best Friend

I hold out both hands, on each a beautiful ring.
Choose, I say to our family friend,
which ring you want to wear today.
Twenty-five years old,
out as a woman for far fewer,
I am helping initiate her into the mysteries
of quality women's jewelry —
pieces from the secret river
of intimate treasures that flow
through generations of women.

Learning pleasure in beauty that sparkles,
she moves her hand or lifts to the light —
a pinky ring of faceted red.
Places the garnet ring on another finger, and back again.
Lifts the ring to her lips, feels the prongs,
then closes one eye to find rainbows.

Different days she wears diamonds,
emeralds, sapphires, and aquamarines.
She luxuriates in warming gold,
and the moonshine softness of silver.
She is a rare jewel.
Now she knows what that means.

Illuminated

I am pulled from the darkness —
my bed for millennia.
Tossed in camel saddle bags, rocked in boats,
carted and carried,
journeying over five thousand miles
to tumble on the wooden table
of a middle-aged woman
in simple brown wool.

Sunlight through the stone windows
lights her hair.
My blueness, more valuable than gold,
a piece of fallen firmament,
fragment of ocean azure.
I warm in her hands, now raised in prayer.
Slowly, reverently
I am chipped, scraped and ground
into lapis lazuli dust.

Lips part and her pink tongue
wets my blueness, suspends me on her brush.
I am stroked, laid down and pressed
into sacred contours
as I become blue shadows in angels' wings,
and heaven, holding a golden comet.

My greatest joy — to transfigure
the cloak of the Virgin Mary
and accept fervent kisses from the faithful.
Particles of me descend back into darkness,
buried with her —
she who illuminated my passion.

After nine hundred years of silence,
her bones are discovered and unearthed.
Archeologists detect blue rock dust
imbedded between her teeth.
We rise from the earth to live again.

Observance — Easter, 2020

My desk looks out over
our wooded neighborhood park.
Trees afford a sense of privacy
for walkers, forest bathers.
Light off the ocean silvers my window.
A fine coating of yellow pine pollen
dusts the glass.

I observe, unobserved —
panting dogs eagerly treeing squirrels,
occasional workmen pissing
against a Monterey cypress,
laughing teens smoking dope,
and lovers pausing for a kiss
in a vermillion sunset.

Early, on a quiet Easter morning,
the house sparrows are barely awake
just beginning to peep in light mist.
A thirtysomething woman appears
dressed in running clothes.
On her brown curls,
a floppy set of pink and white
bunny ears.

She runs a circuit of loops
on the trail in our small park.
Every time she reaches the top
of the modest wooded hill,
she stops and hops.
Her hands curved in little paws.

It's a kind of desire

After The Patience of Ordinary Things
— *Pat Schneider*

How the molten basalt yearns for the sky.
Crows fall into the arms of the wind.
Hot sun coaxes dampness from my skin,
as white pine trees rise.
The passion of a honeybee
in a foxglove bloom.
How waves caress sand, again and again.

Rain

The atmospheric river deluges
our San Francisco neighborhood.
The wettest day on record for October,
near hurricane-force winds.
Pacific winds slam the park's numbered trees.
Whips them again and again, roars.
Sky-sheets of rain flung sideways.
The house sways and rattles
like a clipper ship under full sail.
The Golden Gate Bridge wails in the gale.

In the sodden, becalmed morning-after,
needles and branches litter tarmac and grass,
broken limbs dangle.
Fallen Monterey pines sprawl down hills, block paths.
Torn roots tip skyward and dirt caves yawn.
The ocean is white with high surf,
kelp tossed up and half-buried by new sand.

Downed trees are like beached whales.
Exposed branches, flesh, untouched by humans.
Where only ravens, hawks and squirrels trespassed.
Pine trunks smashed, crowns broken.
Thicket of a crow's nest ransacked,
wedged between crushed boughs.

San Francisco Parks and Rec tends the trails
but leaves these trees as they died.
Toppled by forces of change,
offering refuge to new seedlings
and a lesson in humility.

Starting A Quarantine Project

Silver flowers with mother-of-pearl petals,
lapis lazuli and inlaid leaves.
In the center, a circle of abalone,
an Earth or mandala.

Every day, I select a different brooch
from my inlayed box of jewelry.
Stick the sharp through my fleece,
flip the catch. Smooth my hair.
Document with a photo.
Note its family provenance.

I curate my mother-in-law's collection
of cunningly carved, painted birds,
crosses and golden lockets.
My matrilineal legacy
embraces pearls and diamonds.

A crescent of Victorian seed-pearls
cradles an enamel bouquet
of blue forget-me-nots —
a gift for my mother from her parents
when she graduated, class of 1927.

Tomorrow, I will slip the oval cameo
from its pouch of old chamois.
Gold ivy frames the conch shell carving,
a shepherdess with crook and sheep
pausing under an elegant elm.

Someday these jewels will be my daughter's.
Possibly sooner than later —
as I scan COVID-19 news
three weeks into shelter-in-place.
In New York there are make-shift morgues.
I don't want to wait too long
to enjoy my turn to wear Grandma's family jewels.

My Daughter Sleeps a Lot

She is not alone. Around the world,
young and old with long COVID sink
desperately onto woven mats, sofas,
futons, and car back seats, to dream.
Tired even after morning and afternoon naps.

Between sleep times, she knits
intricate scarves, cowls, leg warmers
in magenta, sea glass, cobalt and rose
from merino, silk, linen, and alpaca.

Her fingers mirror the work of her brain,
knitting together neurons and damaged cells
from the dysfunctional COVID dance
between immune system and virus.
Neurons will inevitably stitch back
into different designs, unexpected.

She is not alone.
Family and friends, give her time,
tuck blankets around her on the couch,
share uncertainty and hope.
Thank her for her knitted hugs.
All know themselves changed.

Give Us a Sign

> *Based on a July, 2022 scientific report from*
> *National Oceanic and Atmospheric Administration.*

Over a mile beneath the Mid-Atlantic Ocean
benthic cold, dark, seemingly barren
dust flats stretch out like deserts.
Yet the submersible finds rows
of perfectly spaced hole-like slits
in the empty sea floor.
Unimposing, totally unexpected
and thoroughly unexplained.
It is designated *lebensspuren* or "life traces."
Not geologic or some artifact
of deep sea currents, but tracks
of something alive.
Marks, writing for us to ponder
like silvery ghosts of snail trails,
or invisible webs
briefly strung with diamonds of dew.

In the pandemic sadness of days,
her face weighted down by dark clouds,
shows the trace of a smile.
Lebensspuren.

Hawk Shadow

Late morning no fog,
breezes off the ocean still gathering.
My eyes catch shadows
as they slide up trees, across grass and road —
hawks, crows, ravens, titmice.
Half-second glimpses of wings
flicker.

Plane shadows blink by too fast,
unless I am on top of a mountain.
Perhaps I imagined a silhouette
on the underside of a cloud.

Nightmare shadows fade in the rising sun.
If only I could imprint birds' flight on silk,
like the leaves shadow-painted on my scarf.
The hawk's swift soar
remembered as afterimage,
as my spirit will some day, fly free.

Duty Calls

This man parks his black SUV neatly at the curb
of the small, wooded park I see from my desk.
He steps out, slowly untangles his music cord,
pulls on stretch black gloves, methodical, precise
as he looks out into the middle distance.

He doesn't see me or the mist-filled trees.
When he opens the hatch of the Mercedes,
the aged golden retriever eyes the jump,
pauses, makes it, a little unsteady.
The man stares away, leashes the dog,
who doesn't look at him either.
Dog's tail wags slightly,
like a required queen's wave
after seventy years of reviewing troops.

Back soon, only time for one circle of the tiny park.
The man unfolds a fancy set of folding stairs
for the dog to climb into the car.
But first, he takes a folded, white towel, dries the retriever,
and carefully cleans each leg and paw.
He lifts the white gold legs a little abruptly
so the dog has to shuffle to stay balanced.

No words. No eye contact.
No pat on the head as the hatch slowly closes.
Before driving away, he sips his coffee,
carefully replacing the shiny tech bottle in its holder.
He will repeat the dog chore
at 2:30 in the afternoon, sharp.
Please save me from such a relationship.

Jasmine Tea

Rolled balls float languidly in hot water
expanding into long curved leaves.
My glasses steam as I lean over
the crackle glaze cup.
Far from my morning kitchen,
steep hillsides unfurl in my mind
as I inhale the scent.
Early sun touches serpentine rows
of waist-high bushes.
Taiwanese mists dissipate
into the gray-white sky
as they drift up tea bush covered slopes.
Down-slope, acres of jasmine.
I want to stand in the midst of those flowers
— and breathe.

Know My Place — Noon

Inauguration — January 20, 2021

Two petite daffodils — pure essence of yellow
with a smell of heaven and early spring.
These are the color of Amanda's
wool coat. A sprig of crocosmia
is her crimson headband.

Air in the garden is lighter, my breath
easier. I believe again in hope, vaccines,
the future of our planet,
goodwill, and good intentions.

The potted buckeye tree,
a seedling gift to my daughter
from her preschool teacher,
is almost ready to crack open its buds
and unfurl soft green fans.

I want to suspend this tenderness of hope
the way the hummingbird hovers near my face
in a quiet vibration of wings.

Self-Quarantine — February, 2020

Just us, coughing,
laughing, sleeping in our house.
The open living room-dining-kitchen
has become a walled off cave, an anchorite's cell,
an air-raid shelter, Rapunzel's tower.
Buried alive yet floor-to-ceiling windows
show us a pale blue sky
and circling red-tailed hawks.
Flirting, iridescent hummingbirds
streak past, climbing and diving.

I make key lime pie and take a nap.
Next day, I write a poem,
do a load of dishes, rest, drink tea.
Laundry, always laundry.
Bake banana-coconut bread.
Discuss merits of various expectorants
and how to pronounce guaifenesin.

We play video games —
Magic, StarCraft, League of Legends.
Answer the door for delivery — Thai food.
Read the history of chess pieces
or tales of 11-year-olds in a strange world
of talking weasels and frog trees.
Scan medical articles about the coronavirus.
Boycott the State of the Union.

Border Skirmishes

You perch at your ease in my garden,
balancing your soft rump on a frail branch,
long tail swinging or curled for support
like an English lady at tea, hand on her cane
as she leans over for a sugar cube.
You take a polite bite of lemon rind, savoring.
Ah, you say, last season's Meyer. It was a good year.

Damn you rats for polluting my lemon tree,
strewing your hantavirus pellets, carelessly
leaving trails of disgust and disease.
I pay the water bills, fertilize monthly,
prune, pamper and swoon over the sweet scent.
My arms show the pruning scratches from citrus thorns.
And you, you ultimate freeloaders, rogues,
mooch, steal and vandalize.
I am defiled, invaded and defenseless
against your nighttime raids.
My teeth grind and my fists clench,

Ultimate insult — a cellar incursion and occupation.
My eyes fill with tears to see my daughter's
boxed yet beloved stuffed animals
massacred, mutilated, urine soaked.
Rats have stolen sweet
reminiscences of my baby's smiles,
talcum powder and night lullabies.
Now, I must trash the dead pink bunnies,

eyeless kittens and gnawed turtles.
If only the stuffed animal dragons,
wolves, panthers and orcas could fight back.
They would make quick snacks of you all.

Those careful holes nobbled in cardboard boxes
are entry doors to your warm nests.
You are smart, curious and playful,
like my daughter.
My jasmine vines on the stairs are a jungle gym
for your babies. No fruit, just fun.
I know you by your calling cards.

An unpleasant part of our urban creature family,
you disappear and return like a bad penny
when the weather turns and the fruit ripens.
Scrabbling, slinking your way inside
if I leave the garage door open by mistake
or a gap anywhere as small as a quarter.
I startle awake as air vents or walls creak
imagining paws and tails, fearing the worst.

I admit, I must honor and thank
your cousins in laboratories
who have saved human lives,
often at the cost of their own —
after being tortured, Frankensteined,
cloned and infected.

My niece kept two pet rats.
Cute when clean, coats like tiny Dalmatians,
scented of pine shavings,
they perched on my shoulder,
whiskers tickling my ear.

I'll set that against your account,
but you still owe us for the Black Death.

Neighbor Kids With Screwdrivers

COVID-19 flew over the ocean, skipped borders,
hid in our lungs, rode-along on delivery packages —
we feel the compactness of a connected planet.
We stare at maps and videos from China, India, Iran.
Watch an elderly gentleman explain in Italian
how to make sanitary napkin face masks.

We walk each day past children playing in the streets,
children we only saw before, getting in and out of cars.
A third-grader loudly excavates with hammer
and screwdriver, the outcropping of rippled bedrock
in our local park, a hands-on science activity.
She searches for fossils, brings home rocks,
becomes a Michelangelo in her imagination.

Parents and children set out on scavenger hunts,
stalk invisible bears, curl on blankets
spread over damp grass, spin fairy tales.
I can hear their shouts and songs over
newly quiet streets and skies.

Ties That Bind

Mom, do you want to learn how to knit?
I put her off for a couple months.
My daughter is an architect of wool,
a choreographer of fibers improvising patterns
and 3D presents for family friends —
scarves and cowls, half-gloves, hats and halters.

Her fingers weave so fast the house is strewn
in colors, hanks, and skeins.
Merino, alpaca, silk, and cashmere,
mohair, and qiviut —
recycled, upcycled, organic, free trade,
local sheep, heirloom goats, combed angora rabbit.
Dyed with indanthrone blue and woad,
dandelion root, acorns and goldenrod,
into yarn named blue pinewood,
steel smoke, kitsune or pool of tears.
Yarn heathered, marled, and worsted.

We agree on wool (Targhee), color (Homemade Jam)
for spiraled legwarmers to warm my calves on cold nights.
It's time for her to teach me to knit my own.

My brain stumbles like my feet
learning to line dance.
Halting, observing, holding, not too tight.
I watch her. Fumbling.
She watches me. Patient.
My thumb gets numb.

I loosen up.
We sit, shoulder to shoulder
laughing on the couch.
Colors moving, needles clicking.
Our fingers turning in step.

I was the person at the wedding

Based on a true news story early in the pandemic.

Who infected one hundred and seventy-seven people.
So far, three dead.
Yes, we should have all worn masks,
but that didn't happen.
Each person decided for themselves.
It's not all my fault.

The event at the Big Moose Inn was lovely, intimate,
only sixty-five guests. I knew she wanted to keep it small.
Dancing was energetic, shrimp and lobster scrumptious.
They had my favorite, a Princess Cake.
The miniature bride and groom
kissed atop the green marzipan icing.
The Atlantic Ocean glittered sun blue.
My ex-best friend from high school glowed
as she slow-danced the first waltz with her new husband.

I guess I am responsible
for poisoning their memories.
Her wedding will be a story
that everybody tells.

My funny uncle that I hadn't seen in years
until the wedding?
I will not visit him in Texas, after all.
He joins me every evening as one of three ghosts

who sit on my bed.
A boyfriend from high school
I broke up with in our senior year —
we are together now forever, ironic no?
The Millinocket librarian is the third wraith
in this inverted Ides of March triumvirate.
She wasn't even at the wedding. Not my fault?

Perhaps I'll choose to join them soon,
but not by COVID, apparently.
I was asymptomatic,
except for those sniffles I thought were allergies.
Pestilence, that Horseman of the Apocalypse,
just galloped by me, laughing.
Following close, the Grim Reaper.

Fox News, 2020

Someone left their Christmas tree
in the park outside my window.
I am greeted daily by views
of successive waves of dogs and their people
come to this wooded city park
for fresh air and a chance to slip their leashes.

Various posts and trees hold
special nose interest
but the canine nasal scrutiny
of this overturned pine is extreme.
Retrievers and pugs stop
and begin to minutely examine this artifact
with attention worthy of Sherlock.

I would love see the scent colors
and data streams of dog perception
overlaid on our visual landscape.
Like the monochromatic, quiet flowers
that shout-out their insect come-ons
in ultraviolet humans can't perceive.
We miss whole channels of communication.

This discarded Christmas tree is telling spaniels,
poodles and mutts something extraordinary.
Perhaps coyotes have added messages,
though that would hardly be news anymore.
There have been mountain lion sightings
in the city since the pandemic quiet.
That would be an arresting story
of anxiety and intrigue.

Annunciation

Like a tiny kazoo,
a bumble bee is deep inside
a foxglove blossom.
The bee rubs bristles against flower fuzz
on the fuchsia runway into nectar.

The spikes of foxglove lean against
my fence and English cottages.
Innocent in appearance, yet in titration,
it is a heart medication, or poison — digitalis.
All in measure. Life and death.
All in timing and intent.

My day lilies, geraniums and violets
profligately seed, bud, or daughter-plant.
I feel heartless in Spring
as I prune or yank sprouts
and toss them on the compost pile.

I am a Goddess in Spring,
planting sage and poppy seedlings
to take root, unfold leaves, and flower.
Bees nurture their broods with the sweetness.

Stumbling through our lives, we try
to hear the words in the hum.

Revelation

He walks through the empty park among tall pines in the pandemic stillness. Their baby is secure in the front facing carrier, a white billed cap on the small head. The baby's mother, his wife, is in the ICU with pneumonia, fighting to get enough oxygen. They are not allowed to visit her. With family medical leave and no working from home, he suddenly has all the responsibility to be with the baby. Despite anxiety for his wife, he enjoys this daily outing with their child. The air smells fresh. He walks on damp earth and leaves, pauses to run fingers over the bark of trees. Hands tiny daisies to the child, who tries to stand, kicking both feet in delight. Even though he knows better, he crumbles snack cereal for scrub jays and pigeons. The baby gurgles and laughs at the birds, head turning to the sky to follow their flight.

Even the thought of folding clean onesies, sweeping the floor, and singing songs to the baby gives him joy — more than he felt on the best days of computer programming. It had been a while since he was thankful at work. He wants his wife healthy, home and in his arms.

She is a doctor, born to it. He loves her for her passion. They knew she was running a greater risk of getting the disease. Both were already irritable with lack of sleep, fear, and overwork before she got sick. Even the baby was crying more and fussing a lot then. What will happen when she gets better? In the middle of the night, up to heat milk, he feels the tension leave his shoulders. Now he knows.

> A baby, a pandemic —
> a mother's hospital window
> the circle of blue sky.

The Guardian

A white dog with black paws,
sharp nose, pointed ears, coat sprinkled with gray,
looks me in the eye. Greets, sniffs,
and ambles away.
In her sight and warm breath, I pass a test.
My heart is weighed and found enough.

The dog's family house is seaward
of our wooded park.
Out the second story window facing the street,
a narrow flat roof.
Many days, the dog lies there on her round bed
in the sunlight off the ocean, as if curled by the hearth.
Watches us like an old man rocking on his porch
or a ruined castle gazing out to sea,
settled on its promontory for centuries.

Occasionally, an older woman climbs out the window
to read at the tiny cafe table, her friend at her feet.
They both look up to see cars pass, other dogs,
and children playing tag among the trees.

I want to see through that old dog's eyes,
smell the wind through the Monterey pines
and the ravens' wings.

Blue-Lavender — Afternoon

What's Next for Me?

Thanks for asking.
Ok…if I am very lucky,
I've got 20+ years left.
The question seems odd to me now.
Strange — planning was my career.

I'd like to walk in maple woods,
stop to lift a leafy pulpit for a look at Jack.
Suck a stem of sassafras,
crumble mint leaves in my pocket.
Smell coffee beans
poured like tropical rain
into the whir and grind at the roastery.
Tag passages in poetry books
that bring me tears.
How about I sketch a slipper orchid
with blue India ink?

How about I listen to you?

A Welcome Visitor

The sofa growls sleepily.
She rolls and shifts sliding deeper
into the cushions.
With the green crocheted throw over her head
six feet, five inches of human disappears,
becomes one with the oatmeal-textured couch.

She has it bad. We all do.
Sleep in the pandemic assumes a character.
Not merely a matter of hygiene,
like teeth-brushing,
but a good friend who comes to visit,
or maybe a partner.
I snuggle into the warm spots
my husband leaves as he rises from bed.
Eyes dropping slowly closed
as I invent garden designs,
poem phrases, new recipes
I don't ever remember
but seem, at the time, just right.
Throughout the unwinding days,
every emotion is tinged
with shades of tired or slow, heaviness
at the back of the eyes.
Heads loll over fantasy novels.

Daily meditations turn into cat naps.
Sometimes we stay up later in the evening,
schedules confused.
Mid-afternoon, strange dreams drop by.

But at the end of the day,
we are always happy to share
our time with this friend.

My Chinese Elm Bonsai Is Family

And that makes my dereliction worse.
I forgot to water it enough.
My excuse is every pandemic day is like the next.

The crown of the tree has no leaves.
Not the deciduous drop of winter.
This is summer, hot and hotter.

COVID paused, I take it to the bonsai doctor.
It is root-bound, coiled tight, unable to taste water,
nutrient starved. A bit like me stuck in the house.

New pot, pruned and planted, I replace it on the porch,
push other pots up around to huddle
for shade and humidity.

It is thriving now. Emerald lush leaves
— but only on the lower boughs.
Gnarled top branches will never re-sprout.

The tree is far from dead, but holds its damage.
My daughter's collar bone has a steel plate.
I have two metal femurs and hip sockets.

The pandemic will leave us changed.
Bonsai's sister art, kintsugi,
mends broken bowls with gold.
I will keep the dead branches.
Shape the tree to celebrate our resilience.

Grandmother

An ancient pug-bulldog mix
with splayed hips
tries to drag his legs through the grass,
out to do his business.

His master, my neighbor,
is a young man with young children
living in the debt-free house
of his dead grandmother.
I suspect the dog was hers.
Now he honors her with patient kindness.

I try to tell if I can see pain
on the dog's serious, wrinkled face.
I suffered such discomfort
before my hip replacements.
Does Louie feel the same?

He turns his flat face to peer
at his master with a trace of bewilderment.
Perhaps he remembers
running with a terrier or dachshund
only a few yards away in the dog park.

The sun is out, the day gentle.
After helping him down the curb
his master lets Louie set the pace
in his slow, swaying walk.

The gray-whiskered dog hobbles
to the edge to sniff curiously at a weed
and blink up at the horizon.
Still not ready to turn back.

Retrospective: Pandemic Days

Every day, I drive the same roads.
Shadow triangles of pitched roofs,
crenelated patches of darkness,
projected on the asphalt.
In morning light,
jagged, sawtooth
silhouettes of side-by-side houses.

Dangerous to drive over
these shadow cliffs.
I might hit a drop-off
and fall
through ocean edge-railings.

But the road is smooth.
The pointed chasms pass through me —
dematerialize like the angel of the Lord
as ragged pitfalls yawn
in the rear-view mirror.

One day, sadness —
the projection of shadows,
fills me, consumes me and I dissolve.
The next, I am impervious
to darkness.

Keep driving.
Don't look back.

Breaker Zone

The passage of windy gusts
rolls through dry winter grasses.
Light shadows waver
beneath tall Monterey cypress.
Branches sway
like kelp caught in swells.

There is a simplicity for some,
in pandemic times —
a purity of life in seclusion.
A barnacle in a shell, I wait.

The contagion crests and crashes
only to rise and roll in again.
All is *de minimis* against the undertow
of uncertain death and disease.

Grace

The pseudo-Tudor house is old-leaf brown.
Mottled sea-fog dusts the stucco,
crisscrossed by beams of tree-trunk black.
Drying bushes, covered with soot and exhaust,
huddle near steel-gray stairs, curb-close.
All glimpsed at a streetlight pause.
Rising from the dusk
in full bloom, one golden rose.

On Our Forty-Ninth Wedding Anniversary, We Do Family Therapy

We arrange two rows of two chairs
in front of the screen
so the therapist can see us all.
My husband and I are in the back,
our daughter and friend,
living with us for the duration,
sit in front.
As it should be.
They careen into the future.
He and I hold the past.
All live in this pandemic now.

We are stuck on a spaceship,
NAV/COMM down, no way to get off.
Days pass at lightspeed, yet feel motionless.
A blended family in the pandemic.
Negotiating agreements for seeing friends,
putting away late-night dishes,
sharing what we learn from trauma.

We devise a system of verbal lights
to manage conversations/questions/requests
energy levels/anger/fear/overwhelm.
Yellow Light means — *Stop very soon.*
RED Light — *Stop, now. Please.*
BLACK light — *I am walking away.*

We learn to share our appreciation,
gratitude, warmth for help
with stories and computer issues, drives to lattes,
jokes, soft sofas, red velvet cupcakes,
each other's company, hugs.

Good Game! Ready to play again.

Air Under Our Wings

Fort Funston Park nests in sand
at the edge of ocean cliffs
on the brink of the San Andreas fault.
Black-ruffed ravens gather to play
and menace a few Chihuahuas
at the water-dish scrum.
Chat and chuckle with friends on dune ridges.
Steal picnic sandwiches, snag dog treats.

Season of nestlings over in late summer,
adults mated for life reward themselves
with a glorious day at the beach.
It doesn't look like a conspiracy of *Corvus corax*,
but raucous family outings with unsupervised teens
at the Santa Cruz boardwalk.
Groups gather at the sharp precipice,
high above broken rocks and Pacific surf.

With the lift of rising marine air
across their four-foot wingspans,
the birds wind-hover, glide, flip-over,
tumble, taunt and dance
with cousins and gusting air currents.
They display their black-pinioned skill.
Joined, rarely, by humans hang-gliding —
doing our clumsy best
to imagine we too have wings.

Did the Scrub Jay Notice?

Blue-purple haze of the tangled
California lilac bush blazes,
flowers lit by rays of sun
shifting through Monterey cypress.
Bees buzz the small bouquets of flowers,
randomly bumbling their way to the next.
A shrieking scrub jay hops from branch to twig.
She stares at me, shiny black eyes defiant,
head, shoulders and tail
saturated in the same hue of blue-lilac.

Enough

In a fury of rapid-fire cackles and squeaks,
two hummingbirds fight, dive and clash.
Victorious, a miniature green-scaled dragon
returns to brood over its trove —
treasure of the sweet-water feeder.

No time to rest in glory.
Again and again, interlopers challenge.
Two males twirl away in contention,
while a third slides in to sip unobserved.
Aztec warriors wore hummingbird feathers
into war to borrow their ferocity.

The King of this sugar gold mine
can't hoard it for winter,
like squirrels or woodpeckers.
They fight for every sip.
But there is nectar enough for all.
As their Goddess, my bounty
is limitless.
If only they knew.

Tea Ceremony

With the shape of a giant Bosc pear
and an acorn squash's ridged belly,
my silver teapot sits unobserved,
on the highest kitchen shelf
pondering generations of family rituals.

When it is retrieved by my tall friend,
an iridescent dark patina catches the light.
Oxidation and age have painted a frozen aurora.

I polish the pointed conical top
and sleek angled sides to a satin sheen,
fingers blackened with metallic scent.
On a whim, I leave the dark bloom
under its rounded belly
to lick up like blue-orange flames
from between four tarnished feet.

The soft silver reflects a pale blue sky,
pastel petite-fours, salmon dill triangles,
rose flowered teacups, monogramed spoons.
In the metal, our faces are fun-house mirrored —
twisting and faceted.

Darjeeling leaves spooned in,
the steaming tea steeps.
The pot is heavy and hot.
An ebony handle, cool in my hand,

curves into a question mark,
perfectly weighted for me to pour
companionship into waiting teacups.
The task well-remembered from its service
with my great-grandmother.

Howling Up the Coastline — Dusk

I Am a Big Woman Shopping for Bras

I am a bit less humiliated when shopping online.
Not because I am big, but being naked
in downtown fitting rooms is too vulnerable.
Bouquet handfuls of bras
are brought to me by the lady selling harnesses,
or it is architecture? Too small, too pointed,
too push-up, too uncomfortable — not me.
A tiresome, painful exercise
in hugging a positive self-image —
even under florescent lights,
three mirrors, with ill-fitting gear.

I only have a few bras. The old, underwire
bra friend was the sole white one — now broken,
a victim of metal fatigue.
Grateful to shop online, I spend 45 minutes guessing.
Of course, my favorite is no longer fabricated.
When the order arrives in the mail, I bend over to seat
my breasts firmly, as taught.
My mom hooked the clasps in the front
then slid the bra around her midriff to her back.
I am proud my arthritic shoulders can still hook behind.

Essential and friendly, bras are also my second pockets.
Tissue in one cup every morning,
in the other, a single key to the house,
a sprig of thyme or lemon verbena if I am gardening.
Convenient places for lists, credit cards, parking tickets,

a twenty for the farmer's market, my cell phone,
if my pants have no pockets. Women's pants, damn them.
A bra pocket is awkward, but it works.

My breasts deserve my love and support.
They nursed beautifully, when my daughter
and I got the hang of it.
No breast cancer in my mother's line,
but I take them to be squished between the glass plates
of the x-ray machine whenever the odometer says.
I respect them. Take pleasure in their sensitive softness.
Generous, never pert, except maybe when I was 11 years old,
They are not much changed by the indignity of time.
For some people, breasts (I never say boobs or tits)
are their beauty, self-worth — or perceived lack.
My breasts and I have a good relationship.

I ask a lot of my bras —
my companions
morning to late at night.
My breasts, with me all the time.
I know that is not true for everybody.
I wish to say thank you.

Island of My Body

Cold autumn currents crash
against my naked skin,
howling up a coastline
of bays and cliffs.
Hill folds and valleys hide
creeks of secret moisture.
Winter dry grasses cloak eroding soil.
On Lookout Point, the lighthouse
beams its search and call of warning.
Pebbled beaches gather elephant seals and pups.
Gales cough sand to rebuild my edges.
Fog and mist blanket the rocky slopes,
as sea birds, albatross and gannets return.

Cutting My Husband's Hair

First time, it was shoulder length, wavy —
a flag of rebellion.
Next, still mahogany black, with a teacher's cut.
Mine was down my back and autumn-leaf brown.

This afternoon, his hair is the color of falling snow
on newly-turned black loam of potato fields
— those rills of rich dirt he left on the other coast.

I shear his familiar head, leave soft bristles
every shade of black and white —
stippled fox or lynx fur.

Gathering up the pandemic hair clippings,
I toss them off our third-story deck,
where in wind off the Pacific,
the white sheet flaps and billows.

Carquinez Strait

Pacific Ocean winds flow through the Golden Gate,
curve and slide east down the narrow passage
into the Sacramento River valley.

Meets the confluence swirl of tides,
relentless pour of river into the sea,
with the counter rush of wind.

Small, quick waves tremble toward shore
to trip and fall in the shallows.
The water is muddy tea.

Push and pull, a great stir of difference.
Sun sets behind the Vallejo Bridge
and the sky glows raspberry.

Wind blows the color into night.

The Days of Crows

Traversing the larger bowl of valley
that rises to Twin Peaks,
five crows sweep past my windows
to soar, flip, and dive.
Sometimes, they strafe the deck so close
I hear wind-hiss in dark feathers.

Late afternoon, crow school done,
same five, or so it seems,
congregate on branches,
taunt, tumble in the air,
rough-house and tease.
Play their inexplicable games of chicken
with sharp taloned red-tailed hawks.

Darkness rises, cawing.
They join a larger flock, the murder,
fly east in chaotic array.
Spiral and circle the radio tower's armature
before settling down to roost
among the fragrant, rustling,
eucalyptus groves of Mt. Sutro.

Glen Canyon Park

The narrow stream, Islais Creek,
is nearly lost underneath tangles
of brambles, willows, and wild cherries.
Only shadows where there might be water.
Leaf-fluttering rays of light
pick out a robin or junco pecking at berries.

Dragonflies zoom and vanish.
The grind of traffic disappears
at the bottom of the steep valley.
Above my head, eucalyptus trees
climb the sides of the ravine,
shedding their bark in gray-green strips,
covering the soft dirt under my feet
with fragrant leaf litter.

Calls of sparrows, bushtits, towhees
interweave in midday groves.
My fears of dwindling wildlife
are briefly allayed.

Massive logs, in breaks along the trail,
lie in patches of hot sun and mixed shade.
Years of blue jeans before me
have rubbed the best seats smooth.
Two kids and their dad pass by,
each carrying sticks like swords.

In distant glades, I hear children laughing.
A sign tells me coyotes den their pups
in hidden corners under rocky outcroppings.
Late dusk, their songs echo
off the slopes, clearly heard
in houses along the rim.

No street lights and few urban stars
reach down. The night drops
and pools in the canyon,
like dark water.

Metamorphosis

I rub the gray buzzcut
I just gave my husband.
His hair is prickly, yet soft.
Days inch by and lengthen out to weeks,
only to molt and repeat.

If I were a woolly bear,
I would take our hair clippings
to spin a cocoon.
He and I could be wrapped together inside,
adding more nights to the 18,000
we have already spent in our down bed.

After thousands of moltings,
we inch hour-by-hour, day-by-day
toward when we each unfurl
our amber Isabella tiger moth
wings.

Diving Toward the Horizon — Evening

The Young Man Who Died

Clever, inventive, a social conscience,
good son, perceptive, caring and kind,
shy, nerdy — just the way I like them.
Dead at 21.

The neighborhood goes dark,
leaving us in blackness —
sudden, unexpected, unknown.
A delicate champagne flute
smashed to bits on the kitchen floor,
a deer hit by the car.

I expected the bright thread of his life
to be woven through ours into the far future.
Our daughter would be 70, our ages now,
and she would still be
laughing with him, friends with his family.
Nobel Prize winner?
Inventor of world-changing technology?
It was truly possible with this kid.

Why or how — doesn't really matter now.
Unfixable. Dead and gone.
I only want to know
so I can use the knowledge
to try to explain, reassure myself
that it will not be my child,
or yours,
next.

I Thought I Was Immune to the Fires — Living in the City

I hear an electrical arc buzz, see a flash.
Wind off the ocean is rushing class five rapids
swirling around the house.
Wires undulate and crack like bull whips.
Old sea glass green insulators
and bird's nest tangles of wires
cling to swaying power poles.

Electricity sputters off, comes back on.
Clocks blinking, I call the emergency number
of our beleaguered, often incompetent
power and gas company.
After fifteen minutes, the phone is answered.
Two hours later, six trucks crowd
into our narrow, dark, dead-end street.

Yellow-vested men with hardhats, climbing ropes,
and spurs swarm up the wooden pole.
Electricity stays off for hours as they talk and joke
working in pools of night lights
as generators hum.

An alternate reality where sparking wires
catch ancient neighborhood fences on fire,
house-siding blazes, gas stoves explode,
brings tears to my eyes.
We cluster around our dining table
in the yellow light of beeswax candles.
I thought it would be the Big One to get us.

Just For the Night

The sun is diving toward the horizon
through clouds of fire
into the molten heat of magma.

As if just over a volcanic edge,
the caldera
is calling our star home.

Joy Fishing —

The opposite of doom-scrolling.
Thank you, Universe,
for passionfruit milkshakes
delivered to this house tonight
when they were needed
so badly.

Hope Is a Winged Thing
After Emily Dickinson

The dappled air between vaults of old-growth redwoods
is ascintille with ladybugs drifting in sunbeams.
Four alight on my arm, fold shiny wings,
settle to explore and tickle.
Too soon, scarlet carapaces wing away
to rejoin the gentle ladybug currents.

Bugs and spiders, mosquitos and wasps,
infested my rural childhood.
Windshields and car fenders were spotted with carnage.
June bugs battered against our screen doors.
In summer, cicadas chittered like Geiger counters.
Moths flittered, bumping against night windows.

I worry how rarely now
ladybugs visit my urban garden.
Cabbage white butterflies scarce on kale stalks.
Blue ceanothus seldom abuzz with enough bees
for a droning hum.
But my San Francisco chard is munched by aphids.
Ants scout the house in dry season.
Spiders in corners weave and wait.

In the untourished reaches of Muir Woods,
ancient trees and ladybugs continue to dance
their pre-historic gavotte.
Fluttering the downtown high rise canyons,
a tiger swallowtail sips from zinnias,
lays eggs on leaves of the landscaped sycamores.
My hope goes with her.

The Earth Can Outwait Us

Waters of the S'klallam people —
worn earth and rocks stream into rapids
that ripple and tumble into the Strait —
a grind and deep rumble.
Silt and pebbles swirl and sift into salt water
to settle along the ever-growing hook of sand
sweeping into the Salish Sea.

Tucked in the curve of its gravel arm,
the waves calm and salmon fingerlings grow.
Northwest coast red cedar canoes are safe.
The Elwah River has created harbor.
Cruise ships and ferries dock and depart.

Ocean storms and powerful currents
fling stones into the sea.
The rhythm certain and ceaseless.
Earth, water, and air shift the surface
of a planet in constant motion.

So briefly here, we try to make forces
and time hold still.
Patience moves mountains.
The Earth can afford to let us imagine
we are in control.

Invitation

The fog speaks in wet whispers of a drizzle,
with wind whipping tree branches.
It speaks more languages.
Motion, it says. *Direction.*
Sink, heavy — pour.
Dissolve, dissipate and disappear.

It knows itself
to be substance of dinosaur talons,
lava, redwoods, salmon,
glaciers, meteors, and suns.

A circular river
between earth and sky —
You too, it says. *Join me.*

We Imagine Cocktail Bars and Toast Ourselves Around the Dining Table

Found poem in names of cocktails with thanks to bartenders from the Interval-Long Now Foundation, Death & Co's extraordinary book, "Welcome Home" and our resident mixologist, Valerie Laura Jade.

The *White Lady* had a *Cashmere Moment*
in front of the *Decanted Mother-in-law*
turning *International Orange*.
Over in the corner, the *Alabama Slammer*
was going at it with the *Bahama Mama*.
What can you say? *Opposites Attract*.
While watching the *Hanky Panky*,
the *White Russian* dreamt of *Dirty Shirley*
and a *Siesta* — just too much *Stoned Love*.

All this *Original Sin* makes me want to *Bark at the Moon*.
Perhaps I have *Grown to Love Life Too Much* or too little.
It Looks Like Rain. My Paradise Lost, perhaps it is time
for *Early Retirement*, easing down the *Stone Stairs*?

A Midsummer Night's Dream of *Verdant Spring*
would improve my attitude and then I'll be ready
to *Fight the Farm Boys* who are all *Hustle and Cuss*.
I'll be the *Pirate King Punch*, the *Last Man Standing*.

A bit of a *Wisconsin Old Fashioned* and *Awkwardly Tongue-Tied*,
I bow to *Julia Child* offering her a bouquet
of *Sugar Magnolia, Night Wing* and *Dahlias*.
A Hummingbird sips the *Brazilian Orchid*
and *A Honey Bee* settles in for *Sweet Dreams*.

Never Too Old

The man's big hands
bend, shave and weave black ash splints
into a potential of holding.
Knowledge of the tree and its strength,
when the wood will crack or bend —
only familiarity can tell.

Centering with clay
is like a child dancing.
Spinning melted sand,
hot enough to be viscous, pliant,
yet yearning to hold shape.

Transforming mud, trees, sand
into a vase for fennel flowers, teapot,
blackberry basket, ink bottle,
quince bowl and platter.

As I reshape habits that don't serve me,
I touch the still point in spinning time.
Can I yield myself to a new form?
The willow branch breaks.
The melted glass cools.
A wheel of repetition, slow changes.

Haibun for Arachnids

Tinsel strands of the spider web inside our house glint with bits of rainbow. A disorganized web, not spokes and wheel, but a thin thicket stretching from window to sill. Another is half-way up the glass, sturdy in its corner.

Who makes these messy tangles with silk so fine I only see them with my reading glasses? The architects are not out tending their three-dimensional snares this morning. I know they are actively in-residence because sprinkles of little bugs litter the sill.

I learned too much about native venomous spiders, having viewed medical photos of necrotizing bites and fang marks in swelling thighs. My common house spiders do bite but are not very dangerous to humans. I am grateful for another bit of wildness left in the city, in my house, cellar, and garden — a second cougar last month leapt over a fence near 15th and Judah.

I'll probably sweep these webs down, eventually. Spiders create impressive piles of dead gnats. More respectful now, I will use gloves when I clean out the garage, and shake out my pant legs to keep a rare brown recluse from the dark folds.

>   Invisible house spiders snare
>   sun-prisms and fruit flies.
>   Garden spiders embroider webs
>   with dew-diamonds and silken death.
>   I live with exquisite predators.

The secret of the universe

Is in the fawn fall of my daughter's hair,
the streaming tail of an icy, unexpected comet
and a black dog with one white knee sock.
In the laugh of a coyote at twilight,
a crumpled bay laurel leaf,
and whisper taps of fog on my face.

In the certainty of crows and spiders,
the inevitability of shiny beetles in my garden
sliding off their would-be-mates backs,
The surety they will try again.

Humans are curious, flexible,
and we can laugh at ourselves.
The future of the universe
will take care of itself.

Turning Seventy

Another piece of my body cut out.
Instead of being sent to an ossuary,
this part is dissolved into a slurry
with a laser and vacuumed up.
Plastic inserted.
I'll carry it for the rest of my life.
Its twin in my other eye — coming soon.

The cobalt ball of yarn is brighter.
A distant cypress branch yields a secret nest.
The golden light over my sight
like aged varnish on a Rembrandt,
is gone, replaced by a new sun.

Older age is not only living with loss
after loss —
it's also earning a new perspective
and a desire to be kinder to myself.
The time to be curious, study
wild parrots in the neighbor's apples,
listen to tones of bell buoys,
hug my old friends more tightly,
find humor in a new friend's eyes.

Maybe the kindness I feel
comes from greater patience with life,
less need to get things done.
Patience comes to me now,
when my time is even shorter, a surprise.
I can more clearly eye the Burgundy depths.
My glass is three-quarters full.

Unspoken Midnight — Dark

Strait of Juan de Fuca — Port Angeles, Washington

Wind-textured swells ripple
over the Salish Sea.
Morning sun whips wavelets near shore
into a frenzied shimmer
like a roiling school of sardines catching light
on tails and silver sides.

Far away at the horizon,
the undulating coast of Canada.
Cumulous clouds in a huge sky
hover in untidy lines like third grade children
fidgeting in their seats.

Midday lookout from the cliff —
a contemplation on shades and textures of azure.
Spring green alders grow in a tangle
at the border of land and sea.

4:30 brings the barely melodious bellows
of the Coho Ferry returning from Victoria
into Port Angeles harbor.

In the growing line of mist, a city appears, then fades —
a recurrent Fata Morgana mirage
of harbor buildings in Victoria.
Unreal images larger, doubled or even inverted.

As night pours in
sailboats rock in their berths.
The silent lights of tankers and cruise ships
pass by in the Strait
navigating toward open ocean —
miles away through black water.

Swan Valley, Wyoming

Long swells of rolling earth,
unplowed flax and alfalfa stubble
shade from rich brown to bone
in the ripple and rise.

Sky fades into evening,
graying lavender and pale yellows.
Setting sun fires the sagebrush
against jagged November mountains.

Rising at the edge
of the darkening ancient lake bed,
the Tetons guard the silence.
Peaks glow white in the night sky.

Camps, cabins, roads, and farms
barely riffle the surface of the valley.
Years flow, flood and recede.
Seasons turn and fly.

Does My Lineage End If My Only Child Has No Children?

I can choose grandchildren to love.
They might not do engineering puzzles,
like my dad,
or have the same joke-telling smile
of my husband,
or an abundance of freckles.

Chosen daughters and sisters,
and chosen family are precious.
We don't inherit them — we earn them.

I am human, with a touch of Neanderthal,
member of a global family, for better or worse.
I am not so attached to copies
of my strong thighs and brain,
or arthritis and high cholesterol.

Our hugs and tears bind,
spiraling us tightly together.
Love manifests and propagates.

I am getting over this DNA thing.

Red-Tailed Hawk

3:00 a.m.
Rendered in shades of grey,
sharp beak tucked under breast feathers —
she is sleeping.
I watch her quietly.
Feathers slowly lift and fall,
like the sides of a cat curled on my lap.
I am the only one awake in the chill house.
I feel the warmth of the hawk
in the still darkness.
Solid through softness,
two eggs underneath.

Babel

My husband may be getting deaf.
Plugged too much into his earbuds?
Or my voice is dropping quieter and getting higher.
He is having a harder time hearing high notes,
me, my voice — squeaking in age or irritation?

One house down, construction —
jack hammers, electric drills and saws.
What? I can't hear you! Over the shower, toaster oven,
frying, thinking, crinkling, coughing.

When I was a CEO, my days were full of meetings,
always talking and listening.
Time goes by for hours now without a spoken word.
Lunch becomes my only scheduled meeting.
I listen to audio recordings and podcasts to hear voices.

Now, I lie in bed at night
listening to the air filtration white noise.
I hear sentences, conversations, words — just out of reach.
As I slide deeper into sleep,
I know what they are saying.

Deep Night

Drawn up by hip discomfort
and the lighter sleep of older age,
he walks slipper-quiet
to the unused bedroom.
A large window looks out over dark trees
and darker still, ocean beyond.
The setting moon, still in the sky,
is visible below the line of roof
when not hidden by fog.

Tonight, the moon is clear and full,
out-shining the two street lights.
Brilliant rays of moonlight push into the room,
dust swimming in the beams.

Settling on the footstool of the unused armchair,
he gazes out for some time,
the quiet house dark behind him.
Wife asleep in bedroom down the hall,
daughter in the room below.
Around this time every night,
even in rain or wind storms,
he makes his journey.

Midnight Meadow

Inspired by Winter Moon at Toyamagahara
— Hasui Kawase, 1931 Woodblock Print

Winter trees silent
under the full moon, a round
snowball of a moon.
I run through tall grasses.
Crows rustle, hidden in roosts of dark branches,
below indigo pools of sky.
A boulder looms out of wheat stalks,
granite curves sparking in moonlight.
I pause, hand on the silent rock.
Chill water cools my mouth.
Mists, breath, drift upward in cold, clear air.
Wind quiet, I have miles yet to run
through midnight meadows.
All is moon and deepest blue-black.

Teton Range: Wyoming Winter

Dark streams off a young aspen grove.
Shadows of the white columns
draw trajectories on snow.
The powder is quiet — blue-lined
paper waiting for a story or music.

As the sun draws nearer the horizon,
the curves of thin branches
glow in a twiggy nimbus.

Night shadows lengthen and widen,
merging into the evening forest.
The ranks of black trunks
soak in unspoken midnight.

Ode to Doughnuts

Doughnuts — daring me to desire
those hanky-panky curves,
soft, warm, iced O's of surprise,
magic rings to rule.
Saturn's sugar halos and handcuffs.
Sweet fat wheels tumble into boxes,
nestle in crinkling, crumpling paper
from Uncle Benny's Doughnut and Bagel place.
Opens at 4:00 a.m. for coffee, cream and sugar,
dream crunch with a schmear.

Who is up at 4:00 a.m.?
Outer Sunset streets are quarantine empty.
Hungry ocean waves roar.
No pigeons to soar in for peckable crumbs,
seagulls sleeping. Terns don't take a turn.
Golden Gate Park owls distain vegetarian,
not even our coyotes crave crullers.

But raccoons, rainbow sprinkles their fave,
racing fat, striped and waddling,
snatch and grab. Slide chittering
down culverts and midnight drains.
I offer a maple bacon delicious on the sidewalk
and pied-piper-call more nocturnal denizens
from the underground city.
High IQ squeaking and giggling rats
praise their goddess.

Spirit of Mom disapproves with a frown,
but I am statin protected!
A sugar-high rebel with a chakram of sharp steel,
I am Xena, the Warrior Princess.
I ululate with ferocity
galloping through sleepy San Francisco hills
on a wild apple stallion.

I *yippeeee kay yayaaa* for chocolate old fashioneds
not the bourbon old fashioneds of my parents.
French fry edge crunch
trailing midnight chocolate icing flakes
behind me, calling to the ant hordes.

A Quiet Edge

"Return to the quiet edge, those private places."
— *Barbara Swift Brewer*

The Hunger Moon is about to slide full
above the blackness of Twin Peaks.
A Jeep drives the edge road,
silhouetted in front of the rising sandy disc.
Time and space compress to nothing.

NASA Rover feels dust under its tires.
My fingers stroke lunar curves of yellow jasper.
Gray-blue sky pours in behind
as the moon floats up higher
to swim in its lane.
I can taste the stretch of time.

Messengers or Prophets?

A heavy metallic scritching
and loud thump.
My consciousness bursts into the night,
heart stuttering.
Something breaking into the garage
on a hot prowl?
Meteorites? Pieces of space trash?

Scratching of large claws,
a muffled vowel.
Echoing scrape and call.
A trek across our ceiling —
the peaked underside of a shake roof.
My eyes track the stop-and-start hop.
A throaty, low comment.
Tap-tap, rap, squeak.
My brain fires with patterns, language, story.

Dawn wind snags on black feathers.
Meticulous exploration of crevices.
An obsidian eye catches glint,
or bit of breakfast bug.

I don't ordinarily read omens into beaks of dark birds,
what if I dreamed them?
What is the eternal truth
beak-whispered in my ear?

My husband and I are now awake.
Wisps of night dreams dissipate
with the lifting of wings,
ruffling of sheets.

Bodies in Conjunction

Mist rubs pastel into the night sky.
Empty street at 4:15 a.m. — just the two of us.
The eclipsing moon, easily missed,
is modest, shaded.
Shadow of the earth slides slowly
to cover its face.

The lunar disc hangs there softly —
not a paper moon cut-out
but a russet grape, edge translucent.
I feel its roundness, like a tadpole egg,
spherical and full,
star-glow on top, curl of darkness below.

The halo of brightness grows.
We stand wrapped in each other's arms.
The rightness of moon, earth, and sun,
this timelessness, our briefness,
bathes us in a clear pool of night and light.

Acknowledgments

I have such appreciation for my chosen pandemic pod — Fred, Laurel, and our family friend, Valerie Laura Jade. Thank you to my friends and poetry critique group, as well as extraordinary writing workshops by Ellen Bass, Diane Frank, Erin Redfern, Danusha Lameris and James Crews, Kwame Dawes, Robert Hass, Brenda Hillman as well as others who teach and inspire me to keep writing and growing in the craft. My virtual guest attendance at Pacific University's winter 2021 MFA residency was a pandemic delight.

I want to acknowledge the publishers of the following publications in which some of these poems have been or are about to be published. *Fog and Light: San Francisco through the Eyes of the Poets Who Live Here*, as well as *Pandemic Puzzle Poems*, anthologies both edited by Diane Frank; *Love Poems, Volume II* edited by Johnny M. Tucker Jr. Poems from this book were also published in *Vistas&Byways*.

Sincerest acknowledgement and gratitude for the many essential workers, shoppers, health care staff, trash collectors, plumbers and many others and their families who have risked COVID-19 to help me and mine stay safer and more comfortable during this time. I am very lucky and thankful to have had the ability to shelter. To those with long COVID, I wish you hope and health.

About the Author

Heather Saunders Estes (she/they) returned to the arts and poetry after serving 37 years as CEO for Planned Parenthood Northern California and continues to be committed to a lifetime of service and advocacy. The San Francisco Bay Area has been the poet's home for 45 years since moving from small-town New England and Upstate New York. Fog, ravens, and the denizens of San Francisco continue to provide endless artistic inspiration.

These days Heather focuses on advocacy, writing, learning, LGBTQIAA+ and sexual health and bodily autonomy issues, family, friends, native gardening, walking, art, science. 2023 brings the celebration of 50 years of married life with an accomplished writer, teacher and very patient partner. They are the parents of a biologist/writer who is living with them during the pandemic, along with a family friend. It is this experience that led to *All in Measure: Book of Hours — 2020-2022*.

Heather holds a Masters of Social Work and Masters in Public Administration, with a BA in Ceramics and Art Education. Attending numerous summer writing retreats and classes informs their writing, along with the continued support of friends, teachers and the Wild Women Write critique group.

Poetry is an opportunity to experience, examine and share moments more deeply using words, space and music — to put life on pause, feel, discover, and appreciate.

To request readings or speaking opportunities, please contact Heather through the website, www.HeatherSaundersEstes.com where you can also sign up for a monthly poem blog. Facebook Author page is @ H.S.Estes.

Books by Heather Saunders Estes:

All in Measure: Book of Hours (Blue Light Press, 2023)
Cloudbreak (Poetic Matrix Press, 2021)
Inner Sunset (Blue Light Press, 2019)

www.ingramcontent.com/pod-product-compliance
Lightning Source LLC
Chambersburg PA
CBHW030901170426
43193CB00009BA/694